DIARY OF A BROKEN MAN

Nickolas Edward Donovan Thomas

Introduction

You are about to take a trip inside the mind of men. You are about to get the chance to learn the unadulterated truth about your male friends, your brothers, sons, and husbands'. This book is a release of male trauma and the admittance of having a broken soul. At the completion of this book, I pray that the readers gain an understanding of the needs, thought processes, and what is required as a man journeys' to his completion. The hardest thing for some men to do is to admit that we are broken. We find comfort in hiding our truths, which only results in us being mentally, physically, and emotionally drained. There is no turning back now; this is our diary!

Diary Entries:

Boys to Men...4
Alpha Male..11
You Bring Me Joy...14
Those Gun Shots had a Purpose.....................18
Puppy Love...24
A Father's Love..29
Stop Crying Like A Girl..................................49
I'm Broke..55
Who Am I...63
The Roots..66
She Said She's Doing This for Us...................70
Do You Even Want Me...................................76
Why Do Men Cheat..80
She's Going to the Gas Station.......................86
You're Ready, But He's Not............................91
90-Day Rule..95
She's Different..102
You Can Go, but I'm Not Leaving..................107
I Wish I Could Tell You..................................110
Pain Produced Power......................................115
Go Easy On Me...120
How Am I Better...124

Boys to Men

This transition is tough and confusing. My dad was in the house when I was growing up, but he wasn't present. I don't remember talking about saving money, what I should be doing, or learning to become a successful husband. I remember him telling me to go into the Diesel Mechanic industry as a career, but I watched him struggle financially, and we lived in poverty, so my thought was, why would I do something he said when I couldn't see the benefit of his words.

Being what people call a "real man" is hard; you can't imagine the pressure I am under trying to hold it all together. Most of the time, everybody is coming to me so I can help fix their problems, all while I am dealing with my own issues. I'm trying to focus and learn what type of man I will become without the proper knowledge of balancing the forces pulling me in so many different directions.

Most of the time, we think that once we hit a certain age or start paying specific bills, we can start celebrating our manhood. We rush to turn 18 and then run to turn 21 because we think we get a right to passage. The truth is that the rush makes us miss some precious time and important steps that are crucial to our overall readiness for manhood.

Proverbs 22:6 says, "Train up a child, and when he is old, he will not depart from it." That's all well and fine, but we must be careful because what happens most of the time is that a broken man is doing that training. The result of that training will just be the creation of another broken man.

First, we must realize that we are indeed broken. Next, we must identify what caused us to be broken and commit to taking the proper steps to become an overcomer. Afterward, we start to heal and decide what and how we teach the next generation of men.

One day my five-year-old Noah saw flowers growing outside the house. He went to smell them and told me he wanted to give some to my wife. I told him that we would surprise her one day soon. He then said he wanted to give some to his nana also. "I jokingly said I didn't think we had enough money for all those flowers." He proceeded to tell me he had money in his piggy bank on his dresser and how we could use that money to get the extra flowers for my mother-in-law. That two-minute conversation gave me a glimpse into how he was being trained. It showed me that he cared for his mother and saw the value in his grandmother. It also revealed how quickly he could come up with solutions and problem solve as he remembered he had been saving money. I believe that discussion would always remind him of the importance of saving money for hard times. All traits that as a father, I would hope he possessed and multiplied as he journeys to becoming a man.

I did not truly understand what it took to be a "real man" until my mid 30's. The most important thing that I have learned was that if I wanted to continue to have this manly feeling, I had to be willing to admit that I am flawed. I must be willing and ready to consistently mold myself into a better version of the old me daily.

Final Thoughts:

Ladies:

It is not that we don't want to be the man you want us to be; we sometimes just don't know-how. The male in your life might have been robbed of some valuable time. A time that he would need to truly learn how to be the man that you seek, a man that could make you happy forever.

Men:

We have to do better. We must stop making excuses to live in the boy version of ourselves. We have the power to right our wrongs; we have to stop validating our wrongdoings and messed-up beliefs. We have more to offer to the world, and the only way we can take our rightful place is if we learn that becoming a man is a journey, not a race.

Alpha Male

The biggest, strongest, and most respected in the jungle. Nothing can happen, and there is no peace unless he says so. I'd be crazy to give that up. It's the reason why every male in my eyesight is sized up. Not because I want to but because I must. I'd kill to protect my territory; I'd die to ensure my family is safe and eats. There is no limit to what I am willing to do to hold the title of the alpha male. So it's not that I am violent, but I damn sure am not willing to give my title or territory up to someone I see as lesser.

I've struggled for so long with this, overly triggered with males. I even have thoughts of killing them just for them looking me in the eyes. I love my family so much because having them in my life has honestly saved so many people from me, but most importantly, my family saved me from myself!

Final Thoughts:

Ladies:

We need you more than you or we even know. Naturally, we are protectors, and we are willing to do whatever to make sure you validate that we are an alpha male. Help protect us, let us know that everything is alright. The best thing for an alpha male is for his queen to put him at ease.

Men:

All is well; people don't really test us too much anyway; we are just paranoid. Settle down and enjoy the peace of your space. Colossians 3:8 says to put off all these; anger, wrath, malice, blasphemy, and filthy communication out of your mouth. Change is good; you are worth more roaming your jungle than buried in it.

You Bring Me Joy

Sometimes, it is hard for me to find joy in a world where everything seems to be against me. I know I have to make myself happy, and I do, but that does not really bring me joy. I also know that I am supposed to find joy in the LORD, but I have gone back and forth with that relationship for so long that it does not feel fair to ask him for the favor of giving me joy. That means sometimes I walked around with the biggest smile and the saddest soul. I am hurting and searching for what would truly bring me joy.

So, what is joy? Well, the definition says it is a feeling of great pleasure and happiness. It has to be deeper than that because that would mean that joy could run out as soon as I wasn't being pleasured or something caused me not to be happy.

The bible says that joy comes in the morning in Psalms 30:5. To me, this means that joy is a position and a decision. You see, joy is something that only the LORD can bring. Once you receive that understanding, you must mentally position yourself at a place of peace where you understand that everything will be alright by faith and with him. Once I decided to trust and walk with God, everything in my life opened up, and I started to feel free. I could fill the voids I had in my life closing, and I no longer felt empty; temporary feelings of happiness also began to leave, and I began to find eternal joy.

Final Thoughts:

Ladies:

Being with my wife brought me happiness, but it wasn't until I grew spiritually that I found joy. It wasn't until I stopped playing hide and go seek with the LORD that I stopped allowing temporary pleasures to rip our union apart. You will not find joy in a man until he has found joy in the LORD.

Males:

What brings you joy? That question might take some reflection, but it is super necessary to find that answer. As you reflect, don't confuse happiness with joy. Happiness can be controlled by others, but true joy comes from the LORD!

Those Gun Shots had a Purpose

I am lying in bed, taking a nap, and I hear a strange sound outside of my window. I know nobody is testing me like this! I look out the window, and somebody is breaking into my car for the second time this month. This time would be different; the first time, I had to assume, wait, didn't I leave money in the armrest? Did I leave that open? This time, I didn't have to wonder because this bold idiot was still inside my car. He must not have known who's car he was in, but he was about to find out. I had been waiting for someone to violate me enough to make me take their life.

I wanted this street credit under my belt, and I was about to get it. I grabbed my gun and ran out my door only wearing underwear. As I approached my car in broad daylight, I screamed, "it's over for you," the robber saw me and took off, running down the sidewalk parallel to my neighbors' fence. Pow, the first shot missed, I ran to try and get another shot, pow, the second shot missed as well, pow, the third shot misses as the robber turns the corner, ducking and running. I go inside, grab my car keys and young son and begin to drive, looking for where he had run off to. I was going to kill him that day. I wanted to so badly, but honestly, I don't even know why. My adrenaline sometimes gets the best of me. I had no other thought other than to prove to them all that I would do it, that I shouldn't be tested. I don't even know who "them all" even was.

Those gunshots made me realize how I was riding around looking and ready to get into a shootout with my innocent baby in the car. What had he done to deserve to die if things went wrong? All because I loved the feeling of rushing adrenaline. I was sick, a menace to myself, living life on the edge, reckless, and without regret for my life or others. I wasn't even responsible, playing Russian roulette with my life, and I didn't even have insurance on myself so I wouldn't be a burden or cause my family extra grief if I died.

2 Corinthians 5:17 says that if any man is in Christ, he is a new creature; old things have passed away; behold, all things have become new. I have learned to value my life more. As I journeyed to finding my purpose, life has become more filling. I have now found creative ways to control and use my adrenaline for the greater good and to serve God.

Final Thoughts:

Ladies:

Learn the extent your partner is willing to go to find pleasure or satisfaction. Is his doings placing your family in danger? Find fun, creative and new ways for him to use his adrenaline. Help him get closer to God?

Men:

It is bigger than you; Don't let your emotions get the best of you and force you to be away from your family. Get insurance for yourself and your family. Not because you are living wrong but because you want to take care of your family even when you are no longer here. Take pride in having everything in order for your family. Wouldn't you much rather have your family receive a big check when you are gone rather than having them start some type of donation account or beg on social media to cover your expenses? Take care of your business as soon as possible. As the breadwinner,

I know it is important that your family continues

to have their bread even after you are laid to rest.

Puppy Love

What is love? Something we tell others to express how we feel towards them. The older I became, I realized that I had no idea what love was. It wasn't a word I used or heard being used much, so I didn't have a proper definition of love. I remember thinking that love was being able to give a feeling of happiness or providing what I thought somebody needed. Doing one of those two things would automatically make them understand that I loved them is the way I saw it.

All of my life, I have loved the wrong way. Not because I wanted to, I just didn't know how to love or what love was. I never practiced how to love or understood that everyone sees love differently. Growing up, I remember telling my mother I loved her, but I can't tell you why I loved her outside of her being my mother. My wife was the first female outside of my family that I told I loved, but I only did that because we were in a relationship, and I thought that was what I was supposed to do.

So here I am, old in age but young in love, and now I'm lost. Struggling to know what love truly is. Remembering how I put conditions on my love and did the same to others. Now I am stuck, looking for love, so I turned to the bible for my answers.

1 Corinthians 13: 4&5 - says that love is patient, love is kind. It does not dishonor others; it is not self-seeking, it is not easily angered, it keeps no record of wrong.

In Solomon, it says that many waters can't quench love neither can the floods drown it.

So now I understand that love is a journey and that true love comes with maturity and understanding. We can't genuinely say we love someone until we are ready to strive daily to show them that we stand by everything the bible says love is. Love removes conditions and looks for value and worth in others. If you truly want to prove your love, make sure you are careful not to pull and take your love away when things go wrong. Love is allowing yourself to be vulnerable even when you think you will be hurt.

Final Thoughts:

Ladies:

He might genuinely want to love you but he can't do that if he is young in the understanding of what love truly is. Until he understands and is willing to go on the journey to mature in the Bible's definition of love, you all will always just have puppy love.

Males:

Learn to love. We must understand that a person's perception of whether we truly love them is ever-changing. The only way we can be perfect in love is to commit to the journey of executing the definition of what love is in the bible. Loving the way the bible says to love allows you to release the pressure of wondering if a person thinks you love them. It also eliminates the excuses for someone not to love you back.

How do you currently express your love?

A Father's Love

I remember when we found out, it was September 17th, 2005. I was so excited; we would be having our first child. Don't even mention the day we found out it was going to be a boy; I spent $1,000 on boy toddler clothes my first time shopping for you. I was ready for a mini-me, someone I could mold and have to carry on my name. I was honored to be your dad; I took pride in letting you lay on my chest as your mother recovered in the hospital. You were mine; I remember the nurses saying they never saw a father as involved as I was with you. I loved you; together, we would take over the world.

At least that's what I thought. What happened to the kid that I woke up to early in the mornings to take my shift of watching you once you came home. Did I ruin that sweet, innocent child that I had, did my love for you force our disconnect?

How come I can't feel your love for me? How come I can't reach you? How come you won't forgive me? Why do you tare my heart into pieces?

    Sorry doesn't fix it all, but you won't even accept my actions; have I not changed? Have I not proved that I love you? This is not what I had planned. A father's love has to be many things, and right now, it has to be distant. Not because I want it to be, but because I need it to be. I would pay any amount of money to have you understand why I did what I did, but I cannot allow you to hold me hostage. The hardest thing I ever had to do was release you. It hurts that a part of me is gone, but your impact on this world is more significant than you know. I trust that one day you will be the person you were always called to be. That you will walk in your purpose and change the world. Until then, I will continue to trust God in all his ways because I know all will be well.

I will love you forever, and you will always be a part of me.

Final Thoughts:

Females:

A father's love is shown in many ways. Before a father can offer their love, they must understand that they can also love the wrong way. Having a child with someone is forever, be sure to discuss the ways your child's father plans to discipline, reward, raise and lead the family. Loving wrong can be costly.

Males:

If the way you loved had words, what would they say? What is your love teaching? Is your love having more of a positive or negative impact? Do you love your family enough to hear that they might feel like you don't love them at all? Is it time to rethink what love truly looks like? Loving wrong can be costly, don't give anyone a reason to say you never loved them if your desire was for them to always feel loved.

The Power-up Love Challenge!

We will learn and reflect on the bible's definition of love for the following few pages. We will dissect one verse at a time and journal our thoughts on what is the true meaning of love.

1 Corinthians 13:1

If I could speak all the languages of earth and of angels, but didn't love others, I would only be a noisy gong or a clanging cymbal.

Reflection

_____

_____

_____

_____

_____

_____

_____

1 Corinthians 13:2

If I had the gift of prophecy, and if I understood all of God's secret plans and possessed all knowledge, and if I had such faith that I could move mountains, but didn't love others, I would be nothing.

Reflection

_____

_____

_____

_____

_____

_____

_____

_____

1 Corinthians 13:3

If I gave everything I have to the poor and even sacrificed my body, I could boast about it; but if I didn't love others, I would have gained nothing.

Reflection

_____

_____

_____

_____

_____

_____

_____

_____

1 Corinthians 13:4

Love is patient and kind. Love is not jealous or

boastful or proud

Reflection

_____

_____

_____

_____

_____

_____

_____

_____

1 Corinthians 13:5

or rude. It does not demand its own way. It is not irritable, and it keeps no record of being wronged.

Reflection

_____

_____

_____

_____

_____

_____

1 Corinthians 13:6

It does not rejoice about injustice but rejoices whenever the truth wins out.

Reflection

1 Corinthians 13:7

Love never gives up, never loses faith, is always hopeful, and endures through every circumstance.

Reflection

_____

_____

1 Corinthians 13:8

Prophecy and speaking in unknown languages and special knowledge will become useless. But love will last foreverReflection

_____

_____

_____

_____

_____

_____

1 Corinthians 13:9

Now our knowledge is partial and incomplete, and even the gift of prophecy reveals only part of the whole picture!

Reflection

1 Corinthians 13:10

But when the time of perfection comes, these partial things will become useless.

Reflection

_____

_____

_____

_____

_____

_____

_____

_____

1 Corinthians 13:11

When I was a child, I spoke and thought and reasoned as a child. But when I grew up, I put away childish things.

Reflection

_____

_____

_____

_____

_____

_____

_____

_____

1 Corinthians 13:12

Now we see things imperfectly, like puzzling reflections in a mirror, but then we will see everything with perfect clarity. All that I know now is partial and incomplete, but then I will know everything completely, just as God now knows me completely.

Reflection

_____

_____

_____

_____

_____

_____

_____

_____

1 Corinthians 13:13

Three things will last forever—faith, hope, and love—and the greatest of these is love.

Reflection

_____

_____

_____

_____

_____

_____

_____

You should have developed a new respect for what love genuinely means. It is now time for you to express what love looks like in your eyes.

Reflection

Stop Crying like a Girl

It always meant so much to me growing up, so I tried to prove it every day. To show my mom and dad that I listened. When I'm hurting, whenever I am sad or going through something, their voices and the words they spoke to me would forever be sketched in my brain.

It made me tough; that was the goal right, to make me a manly man? To help me prove to everyone every day that I am the king of the world. If I fell, scraped my knee, and bled, stop crying like a girl. If I got discouraged and became teary-eyed in my defeat, stop crying like a girl. If I had some emotional trauma and cried while trying to release my feelings, stop crying like a girl.

So as I journey throughout life, I'm perfect at not crying like a girl. I am also perfect at not communicating with anyone, and not trusting that people have my best interest at heart. I'm perfect at not showing my true emotions, and even when people ask how I'm doing, and I truly have something I want to get off my heart, I have trained myself to answer, 'I'm good".

That ruined everything; it forced me to take on the world alone. It makes me believe that I am the only one going through something. No matter what I'm feeling, I must deal with it alone because no one else would understand my thoughts and emotions.

Was this your goal, to force me in a world of millions to feel like I'm living on an island with nobody?

The good thing about being alone on this island is that nobody can see how long I've actually been crying like a girl.

Final Thoughts:

We are hurting our sons, and hurt sons become ruined husbands. It is one of the biggest dilemmas in the world, thinking that we are all by ourselves and that if we want to prove our worth as a man, we can't show our true emotions. These thoughts bring nothing but problems and disconnects us from others in essential areas of our lives.

Females:

- Maybe your relationships aren't working out because your man has been trained to stop crying like a girl. Gain his trust and help your mate understand that he can open up and trust you.

- Are you raising your son to be the type of husband you would want? One that is willing to open up and be sensitive whenever there is a concern. Can he express himself even when it's embarrassing or might hurt your feelings?

Males:

Holding on to the weight of the world is heavy. It is okay to invite others to your island. It might sound cliche but being able to effectively express yourself is more manly than holding it in. It takes courage and guts to pour out your feelings. Putting yourself out there and becoming vulnerable is the first step to your overall victory.

We also don't talk enough! Find a spiritual, level-headed friend who has your best interest at heart. Talk to a pastor or therapist and start releasing some of the things you have been holding in. I promise you will begin to feel better.

Adults:

We have to allow our sons to show their true emotions; it is the only way we can help them. We, with God, have to guide them through their hurts, concerns, and feelings. If their impressionable brains and emotions are not handled with care, the sons we raise will have multiplied issues and end up with crying souls.

I'm Broke

I remember taking baths over the stove. When the lights got disconnected, and our electricity meter was taken. I just went to an abandoned house and took the one from there. We only put the stolen meter in at night because we knew the meter readers were done for the day and wouldn't report it and have it taken too.

That struggle felt like it lasted forever.

After not having the money to pay our bill, our water was disconnected, and that meter was taken as well. We reconnected a stolen meter but the city found out. That caused us to fill up water jugs at relatives' houses with their hose pipes. We didn't tell them that we had even come to their house because our situation was family business! So now that I have money, I'm still mentally broke. I mean, I'm saving plastic forks and spoons, and rewashing paper plates broke.

It's hard for me to forget those dark nights so I try to save everything. Enjoying the finer things in life, but even those are too expensive. No matter the price tag, it's still going to be too high. I mean, I am still going to buy it, but those retail companies don't care about the people; they are only trying to make money. The bible says that the Lord will supply all my needs, but does he not see my bank account? I know he sees that my account is right at my comfort balance. I need him to come and fill this thing back up.

No, I never had anything disconnected or repoed in my adult life, but the demons of my past are very present. But those demons are cast out and die today because I believe your word Lord.

- Your word says, I should take no thought for my life, what I shall eat or drink or put on because birds don't sow or reap, and he feeds them.

- Your word says, that Jesus became poor so that I might become rich.

- Your word says, that wealth and riches are in my house.

- Your word says, that everything I put my hands to will prosper.

- Your word says, that if I give, it will be given. Good measure, pressed down, shaken together, and running over.

I trust you LORD because you have been better than good to me.

Final Thoughts:

Lord, I'm sorry. I'm sorry that I have let my past misrepresent you. I am sorry that no matter how much you gave, it was never enough. I'm sorry that I didn't celebrate you, that I don't allow others to see how good you have been to me, and you have been amazing. I'm sorry that I allowed the enemy to overshadow the blessings and promotions you have provided to me. I'm sorry that my actions caused your words to seem like you are not faithful.

Thank you for erasing my insufficiencies. Thank you for erasing my debt; thank you for blessing me so I can bless others. Thank you for placing me at a point where I only lend and do not borrow.

From this day forward, I am no longer broke but rich and strong in you LORD!

Bible References:

Matthew 6:25-27 - Therefore I tell you, do not worry about your life, what you will eat or drink; or about your body, what you will wear. Is not life more than food, and the body more than clothes? Look at the birds of the air; they do not sow or reap or store away in barns, and yet your heavenly Father feeds them. Are you not much more valuable than they? Can any one of you by worrying add a single hour to your life?

2 Corinthians 8:9 - For you know the grace of our Lord Jesus Christ, that though he was rich, yet for your sake he became poor, so that you through his poverty might become rich.

Psalm 112:3 - Wealth and riches are in their houses, and their righteousness endures forever.

Deuteronomy 30:9 - Then the Lord your God will make you most prosperous in all the work of your hands and in the fruit of your womb, the young of your livestock and the crops of your land. The LORD will again delight in you and make you prosperous, just as he delighted in your ancestors.

Luke 6:38 - Give, and it will be given to you. A good measure, pressed down, shaken together and running over, will be poured into your lap. For with the measure you use, it will be measured to you

Who Am I?

I thought I knew who I was, but the longer I lived, I realized I didn't. Just when I thought I had the answer to the questions of life, it all switched up, and I felt like I was starting over. I know I am growing and progressing, but how come I can't find the answers that allow me to stay in my comfort zone.

What is God trying to teach me?

I know that he made me a warrior, but I didn't realize that when I told him I was ready to do whatever he said, it would take all this!

I guess I'm just a student, someone on a journey to learning who he truly is. Someone who is not his past but doesn't understand what all comes along with walking in his purpose. I trust God, but I am also anxious to see the end results because finding out who I am has been costly.

Final Thoughts:

Finding out who I am will be rewarding for all those who stick around and those who I allow to connect to me as I strive to reach my final destination, but I'm scared. I am afraid I might lose people I love or care about on my way to doing what God has called me to do.

LORD, HELP ME!

Help my heart to see you first. Help those that are dear to me to see your vision for me. Allow them to understand that I am on an assignment for you. Please help them to see my change and allow it to motivate them to find the purpose you have for their lives. Allow your blessings to guide them to finding out who they are in you.

If our lives must be separate, I ask that you continue to protect us individually. Continue to hold our hands and show us the paths you have designated us to travel, even if it's alone.

I trust you Lord, in Jesus' name, Amen

The Roots

How come I can't shake these old feelings, and how come I can't get rid of these old thoughts? Every time I see the light, I become consumed by the darkness. I took ten steps forward, only to be thrown a hundred steps back. You see, that's why I'm physically and mentally drained because something has a hold on me.

I want to be a tree so bad, but I can't stop seeing myself as a seed.

Dark, being drowned, alone, contained in my own skin, and being burned by the thing that was supposed to help me the most.

How come I'm in this position?

As I learned to fight and break through, I was excited about my growth!

My roots went deep and had a grip on everything I did. They were determined to get the victory and erase all the success I had in different areas of my life.

I am worth more than the constant negative trips down memory lane. I am an overcomer. As I reflected and looked at myself in the mirror, I decided that even in my mess, I was worth more. I realized I wouldn't always be perfect, but I was still worth a second chance. I decided that I had to do something so I could break generational curses and help others become a better version of themselves.

I was ready to do something that would change me forever.

I BURNED MY ROOTS!

Now, this is where I want to be, and yes, the grass is greener on the other side. I switched foundations and allowed myself to receive a new support system. My new support system helped me to stand tall and grow. We helped each other fulfill our purpose and live healthier lifestyles. We push each other to reach our goals. We understand that every day can bring a different fight and that one struggle is not bigger than another.

I have never felt this free.

I will never forget my roots; I'm just not connected to them anymore.

Final Thought

I AM AN OVERCOMER!

She Said She's Doing This for Us!

So here we are again, having the same conversation about how I take care of you and my expectations as a husband. I mean, I am into the traditional marriage setup. The wife is supposed to cook and clean, take care of the kids and serve her husband, you know, all those cute feminine things I care about.

Because you are a modern woman, every time I call you "kept," that instantly means it's time for you to jump off the handle. You even went as far as looking up the words " Kept woman," and you rebuttal with how A kept woman has zero bills. Of course, that pissed me off because you do have zero bills unless it's something you created. You know, the thousands of packages that get delivered to the door from shopping because that is all the bills I see. So yes, when I think about your petty little bills, I don't even see them. Besides, we did the stay-at-home wife thing before; remember how you "needed your independence and didn't want to be in the house all day."

Then we talked about you going back to school; I asked you what are you doing that for, and you responded, "I am doing this for us." "So you can help out and contribute more to the house. Did I ask for your help? I don't think so! Is there something we are missing and you are afraid to tell me? Now my manhood is bruised because it's obvious we don't understand the difference between knowing what the other person needs versus what we think they want.

Final Thoughts:

I try to spoil and provide whatever my wife wants and needs. My goal is to provide a worry-free life for her. She doesn't even have to set the alarm to wake up in the morning because I am always up early and want everything in her life to be seamless. The truth is she's more of a modern woman. Nothing I can provide her will fill the empty spaces she currently has. These spaces can only be filled by accomplishing her personal goals and walking in God's purpose for her life.

Females:

It is extremely important for you to understand your husband's expectations for you as his wife. It is equally important for you to express how you see yourself as a wife through your eyes. Don't allow yourself to become so goal-driven that you overlook your husband's actual wants and needs. You might think it will make you all better, but is your husband counting on your accomplishment to bring the family to the next level. Please understand that as you choose your goals, something will be sacrificed. It might be wifely duties, mom duties, friendships, feelings, or sleep but please understand that accomplishing your goals and dreams will be a sacrifice for everyone involved.

Males:

If you want the best wife possible, you have to compromise. You must allow your wife to fill her voids. If you feel things are falling short, have an open and honest conversation about your feelings. Help and support her through her processes. Love is patient and kind, so if you genuinely love her, you will be there as she figures out who she needs to be. Talk to your wife about how you view her goals and dreams. Is it something you see helping the family or her individually? Having the wife you will be most happy with is humbling and brings many sacrifices. In the end, do you love your wife enough to break away from tradition? The answer to that question might be the difference in having a happier wife, who will give you a happier life.

Do You Even Want Me?

This relationship is shrinking me. My ego and pride are leaving my soul by the day. The areas I was most confident in are now becoming a challenge.

WHY DO YOU DO THIS TO ME?

How come I get the feeling that you feel like you would be better off without me?

DO YOU EVEN WANT ME?

HOW COME YOU MAKE ME FEEL UNATTRACTIVE?

The roles have reversed; now you're telling me how I put on a couple of pounds. How come I feel like you're trying to hide me or keep me a secret whenever your friends come around.

Do you even want me?

Months without sex, secret in the opposite room

late-night text. I see how your mood has changed,

and you're all smiley when you come back.

Do you even want me?

Letting me go places alone when you used to go

everywhere I'd go.

People are noticing, and now they are starting to

talk.

I'm starting to hear the whispers of how we were

never meant to be. The good thing about all the

whispers is now, I'm starting to hear how bad other people want me.

Final Thoughts:

Females:

Build him up, the same way you want your partner to notice you. He secretly wants you to notice him and stroke his ego. Let him know that you are still attracted to and want him. That you see his value and appreciate him. Have open and honest conversations about your wants and needs and if you feel they are changing.

Males:

First, don't fall victim to temporary satisfaction. As you start to get the attention you long for from other women, and it will come because that's how the enemy works. Don't hide your true feelings from your significant other; let her know how she makes you feel. Build your confidence in yourself, redefine who you are, and find ways to drown out possible insecurities that might magnify your current situations and emotions.

Why Do Men Cheat?

Wow, that was easy. I didn't even have to do anything except be myself. There was no expectation except to provide her with good sex. I didn't know that excelling at being a man would open me up to all the females that I could handle. She's happy because she sees me as a man of value, and I add completion to the voids she has in her life. I can't believe that she is really willing to share me just to feel validated.

I don't want to do it, but the thrill of having it keeps crossing my mind. She keeps teasing me! You have to show her who you are is all that keeps crossing my mind. Emotions high, I keep getting that roll-a-coaster feeling in my belly. I know it won't last, but the thought of this being only a temporary pleasure doesn't change the fact that I might be about to get pleasured.

I don't even know if I can really even pull this off anyway. Back in the day, when I was in my prime, this would not even be a question. I could have easily made my move and added her to my belt, but I don't know now.

Am I still that guy?

Does she really find me attractive?

Is she really in control, or am I?

I have to go through with it; I need to see who I am!

I'm in a relationship, I know I shouldn't be doing this, but I can't tell my partner what I need and get it. Every time I try to express myself, things get turned on me like I am never satisfied when I'm actually just trying to express my needs and wants. So now I'm holding it in, trying not to hurt her feelings all while trying not to hurt and take my frustrations out on my side chicks' pussy! The lack of being able to communicate shows this relationship's immaturity.

Final Thoughts:

Here is why men cheat; it's easy because there is a shortage of "real men." Men that can at least mentally provide stability or feel voids in someone's life are in high demand. Some women will sacrifice having their own pie for a slice of someone else's.

The Thrill: Sometimes, it's fun to do wrong even if you know someone might get hurt in the process.

Validation: Men want and need to feel validated. He wants to know that he still has it, that the old him is only suppressed but has not disappeared.

Relationship Immaturity: Couples want the perfect relationship but are unwilling to do what is needed to strengthen their union. Instead of effective communication, we develop the thoughts of I can't do or say that. Having limits on how you communicate allows the demons and thoughts that there is something better to creep into your relationship.

Ladies:

You can't stop a man from cheating. The way he doesn't cheat is for you to connect to his soul. Don't give him an excuse to see better in someone else. Understand that somebody else will gladly take your man with all the negative you see and even love the very thing that might be making you unhappy. His true value doesn't even matter; somebody with nothing will see him as something. Continue to be his thrill, and don't let the fire die down. Validate his being, always show him his value and make him feel special. Allow your man to express his wants and needs. Give him the opportunity to express his thoughts and feelings honestly, even if it hurts. Reflect on his words first and then respond.

She's Going to the Gas Station

I took your beauty for granted and not just your physical beauty but your soul. I allowed my discomfort and the feeling of awkwardness to keep me silent. I figured she would know the way I felt. To me, it should have been obvious or I wouldn't be here. I just have a hard time telling you because I don't want to seem too sensitive.

Can she not read my silence?

I look for ways to say or ease it in so she understands it's natural, but then it slips my mind and never comes out of my mouth. To overcome my discomforts, I force finances and try to let my money talk for me. Look at the life I provide, is that not telling you all you need to hear? I really can't see my life without her but It's just hard to express or explain, and over time I started to see her change.

Now she is headed to the gas station. There are plenty of men there ready to tell her how beautiful she is inside and out. Ready to fill her voids and be what I am not.

Can you blame her?

When I was supposed to be building her up, I was secretly ripping her apart.

Do you think I'm pretty?

I am I enough for you?

I was creating a deficiency in my own relationship!

Now they are opening doors, providing the compliments I failed to deliver. She's taken unnecessary trips, not only filling her car up but filling her ego. She told me her needs, and I failed to meet her where she needed me to be. She's happier now, have you seen my wedding ring? My own insecurities forced her away, and maybe I deserved it because she told me over and over again, and I never adjusted. I'm paranoid every time she leaves the house now because instead of me pumping her gas, I forced her to go to the gas station, and they love when she is there.

Final Thoughts:

Males:

They are waiting on her. We have to do what it takes to keep our women happy. Why force her to get attention from somewhere else. You can't blame her if you are leaving her empty. See what they see, and let her know why you picked her.

Don't get comfortable and allow someone else the opportunity to win your girl over. Compete every day to make sure she is getting all she needs from you. If not, let her go to the gas station where she is loved.

Females:

Keep doing what you are doing. Eventually, he will come around, or the man you deserve will be waiting and ready. He will be ready and prepared to elevate you to the next level. As for as your ex, they will be someone else's rebound, thinking how he lost you by letting you go to the gas station.

You're Ready, But He's Not

I know you love to be in love, but when will you wake up?

You can't see that I don't want you?

You keep asking me to go on dates and to spend some time with you, and I keep telling you how I'm too busy.

Don't you know that people make time for what they want?

I see how you try and buy me to prove to everybody that we are going to be together forever. The crazy part is that you are so disconnected that you can't even see that I am not smiling in the pictures and videos you take as you shower me with gifts.

We are on two different pages, you keep talking about marriage and our future, and I keep talking about how good you were last night.

You keep saying how you can't see yourself with anyone but me, and I keep telling you that if I were you, I wouldn't even be with me.

You keep asking about being together on holidays, and I keep telling you how holidays are meant to be spent with family.

I can tell that you're ready, but I am not!

Final Thoughts:

Females:

If you want to know if a man is ready for you, watch his actions and ignore his words. If his actions contradict his words, you could be wasting your time. Avoid falling for his representative; that will be the person you will meet initially. We all have a person that we send ahead of the real us to get us closer to what we really want. Don't ignore the signs that scream we're not ready because you love to say that you're in love, especially when you know that in your heart, you are in love by yourself.

Males:

Honesty is the key; make your intentions clear.

Being honest will avoid unnecessary drama about how she thought you were ready for the next level when it's clear to her now that you are not.

90-Day Rule

Do you think that you can tell how much I am into you by the number of days I'm willing to wait before we sleep together? Do you really believe your worth will increase with me because you hold out?

GREAT, LET'S PLAY A GAME!

You want to be courted, whisked around like a princess. You want to experience the finer things in life. You want to be treated like a lady; you want the doors opened for you as you enter buildings and the chairs pulled out when we go to restaurants. We go on dates, and I pay for everything; you enjoy five-star experiences everywhere we go.

I watch you start to lower your guard, you're ready, but you continue to hold out.
I give even more effort because you're starting to form your own opinion of me and I can tell that you will be ready to give me all of you soon.

What you don't know is that sometimes I get bored and want companionship even if it's temporary. So when I want to have a nice dinner, I call you. When a new movie comes out, I call you;

I didn't want to go to the family picnic alone, so I called you.

Here is what you also didn't know, before I picked you up and after you left. I had the wildest sex ever. You were just a filler. There was no need to pressure you because I had already released my pressure. So I was always good, and now you think I am the perfect gentleman. You are ready for me to meet your family, and of course, I happily say yes because tomorrow is day 90, and we both know what that means.

You sent me your location and asked if I would be free after 9 pm.; of course, this is the day we both have been waiting for.

I shower, put on the cologne you've always complimented me on, grab protection, and text you that I am heading to the address. When I arrived, I could smell the candles burning before you even opened the door.

There is soft music playing, the lights are dimmed, and rose peddles are on the floor leading straight to the bedroom. You begin to tell me how much you appreciate me for allowing you the time to get to know me.

You look amazing in your lingerie by the way!

You tell me how you are ready to give me all of you without limits. I start to undress you and receive the reward of your thoughts. We went for hours.

As the morning rays entered the window and the darkness of night disappeared, I could not help but think how I was about to disappear as well.

You walk me to the door, we hug, and I gently kiss your forehead. That kiss was the kiss of death because I knew this was it, and you would never see me again.

What did you gain?

90 days won't make me do right by you; you can't force me to like or love you if I don't.

Final Thoughts:

Females:

There is a saying that time heals all wombs, but what do you do when it causes one. Do not place a time limit on the readiness to move to the next level. The reality is sometimes we play games to get what we want. Don't allow yourself to be crushed or hurt because of an opinion you form about a person. Be careful to protect your body and mind against men like me.

Men:

We win again, but when will this game be over?

She's Different

I've been with a lot of women, and none with the intent to be there or with them forever. I never lied or committed because whatever the outcome, It didn't matter. I could replace whomever easily. I searched for the greatest pleasure, the least amount of commitment, with the most reward and thrived in staying in that place. Sometimes I might as well have taken the role of a gigolo.

When we met, I had the same intentions. Have sex with her and see how I could profit from allowing her to be in my presence, but she was different.

I believe she knew who I was and how I usually operated when we met. Instead of letting me move the way I normally moved, she pivoted. I could tell that she wanted me but was playing hard to get.

She challenged me from the beginning. My first words to her were," If I give you my number are you going to call me?" " No, but I'll give you mine, and you can call me." She was a savage and sassy; I had to have it.

She was sure of herself; as I gave her my expectations, she countered with some of her own. " If we are going to do this, I'm the only female that can call your phone." I will be the first to admit that my first thought was how much sex and gifts I would have to give up to meet her expectations. I knew I wasn't ready, but I was at least ready to give it a try because she was different.

I felt myself trying to show her that I was the prize, that I was light-years ahead of my competition. At my age, I could be more than a provider. Have you ate today? Do you want to get your hair or nails done? The roles had reversed, and now I was playing for keeps. You want me to yourself, great; now you can never leave.

I said that and meant it. I now owned you, No matter what. I was going to be around forever. I may not have known exactly how, but I knew she was different, and I was never giving that up.

Final Thoughts:

Females:

In a world where people are fighting to fit in, be sure to stand out. Be sure of yourself. The way you carry yourself should naturally make a man want to step his game up. You won't have to force him to change once he realizes that you're different.

Males:

She has options. Don't play around getting dirty with the coal and allow someone else to collect your diamond. Once you realize that she's different, it will be time for you to step up to the plate and do what it takes to keep your prize.

You Can Go, but I'm Not Leaving!

We both knew I wasn't ready, but I tried. Yes, I messed up, which made you leave, but I'm never going. I am always going to be around. We take recovery differently; you're working on becoming a better you, and honestly, a better you for someone else is too much for me. As soon as it looks like you're done with me, I find ways to sneak back into your life so I can have my cake and eat it too. I told you we were forever, and I meant that. I'm not ready to be what you need, but I am also not ready to let you be.

So, we're stuck!

Now I'm trying to control your peace!

Playing with your feelings and trying to control your emotions!

I bring out the worst in you, but you make me better. This shouldn't be this complicated. I tried to trick you by saying we would always be friends, but I only said that to make sure our lines of communication would always be opened. Here is the truth: I don't deserve you, but I'm not ready to see you happy with someone else, so you can go, but I'm never leaving!

Final Thoughts:

Males:

Don't play mind games; you already know what you want. Respectfully tell her your truths. If she is starting to nag, tell her, not fulfilling your needs mentally, physically, or emotionally, tell her. Do not keep your feelings bottled up to have an excuse to cheat or jump in and out of the relationship at your convenience. You already know if you can see forever with her.

Once you reflect and decide if you are really worth it to each other, commit to making it work. Once you commit to the journey of true love, you both will have reasons to never leave.

I Wish I Could Tell You

I want to tell you so much, but I know that I can't. You're going to judge me, and I know you will judge me because I judge myself. There is so much that I want to say, but I'm alone. Trapped, not by you but by all the thoughts I have in my head.

Am I Crazy?

Honestly, sometimes I feel like it. I also feel like the demons in my head are winning. I want to tell you that I feel like it is safer to stay home to avoid the thought of executing others.

- I want to say that I feel like the pressure of being the man you need is too much.
  - I want to tell you that I'm tired of not being your priority, and I feel like we are more of roommates than lovers.
  - I want to tell you that you make me feel like whatever I do is never enough for you, and you never seem to be truly happy.
  - I wish that I could tell you how I believe you have so many talents given to you by God, and I hurt so bad because I watch you consistently decide not to use any of them.
  - I wish I could tell you that they want me as bad as I want you.

- I wish I could tell you that sometimes I just want some time to myself.
- I wish that I could tell you how badly I need therapy.
- I wish that I could tell you to check your attitude; you think I am seeing someone else, but I can't get over the constant disrespect, and that is the real reason I am never in the mood.
- I wish that I could tell you that you keep telling your best friend all of our business, and now she wants to make me her business.

- I wish I could tell you that I want my parents to fight for their marriage because them not being together hurts me.
- I wish that I could tell you that the world might see me as Superman, but I'm really Clark Kent, but I know I can't because if I told you all that I needed to tell you, you would judge me.

Final Thoughts:

Females:

Why does he need to hide or not share things with you? Are you easily offended? Is your connection only physical? Have you all grown enough in your relationship where you can be considered his safe place? The reward of allowing your man to see you as his safe haven is you becoming part of his eternal peace. Once he sees you as that, he will never want to leave that place.

Males:

Slowly tell her your truths. It can be a lot for someone to take in, but the reward for sharing your thoughts and expressions is finding the woman that is truly made for you. As your relationship grows, so will the amount you will be able to tell her and the amount she will be able to help you. Talk your thoughts, and release that extra pressure.

Pain Produced Power

I often asked God why me and thought how a person like me should not even be in this position in the first place. I'm hurting, not knowing if I should go left or right. It looks like I have it all together on the outside, but my soul is beat and bruised on the inside. I can't get any lower than this even if I tried.

I'm in an empty white padded room; it has one window with the greenest grass on the outside. I sit on the floor in the middle of the room, physically in one place but with the feeling that I am running back and forth, crashing into the walls.

I feel like I am a caged animal; get me out of here!

I AM SO GLAD YOU KNOW MY NAME!

As I ran into those walls, I began to pick up speed because I started to feel something stirring up inside of me. I can't explain the feeling, but I can feel that I am becoming numb to the pain.

There is a lesson being learned!

I started to learn how to adjust to the pain; I also overcame the results of the impact of hitting the walls repeatedly.

I am more prepared and ready to take on the result of my next step.

I ran faster because I could feel a change; I could feel the victory.

Faster,

Faster,

Faster, I ran until I broke through the very walls that held me back.

I am no longer captured because the pain produced power!

As I stand in the green grass on the other side, I am thankful for my strength.

I'm ready LORD; I belong to you.

Wherever I go from here, I am moving with your guidance.

Final Thought:

Isaiah 40:28 – 31 says - Hast thou not known? Hast thou not heard, the everlasting God, the LORD, the creator of the ends of the earth, fainteth not, neither is weary? There is no searching of his understanding. 29- He giveth power to the faint; and to them that have no might he increaseth strength. 30

-Even the youth shall faint and be weary, and the young men shall utterly fall: 31- but they that wait upon the LORD shall renew their strength; they shall mount up with wings as eagles; they shall run, and not be weary; and they shall walk, and not faint.

I believe your word LORD, and not because it has proven to be true once, but you continue to renew me daily just like it says.

Go Easy On Me

I'm so thankful for you; I know you didn't realize what you were getting yourself into; even I would not have stayed with me. Ups and downs, being all in and then all out, you were patient with me. With all I did wrong, why did you stay? Nobody would have blamed you for leaving if you told them my truth. You were silent.

I can't thank you enough; I owe you the results of my change. Overcoming being so broken is a journey. One that I could not have done alone, and you were there every step of the way. I had boyish intentions when we met, but now I know that God sent you to me. Did he show you my potential? What makes you stay? I don't even feel worthy of all the love you have shown me, which scares me. If you left today, I couldn't blame you because I'd deserve it.

I promise to continue to grow for you. I want to make everything you endured feel worth it. I'm going to push to become better daily. I can't promise that I will be perfect, but I'm going to try. Lord, why me? How do you get the glory? What made you pick me? I know that I am who I am because of you. You took a broken boy that turned into a broken man and healed him. You never took your love away, never removed your grace; for that, I love you more than anything. I know I haven't been perfect, but I promise to improve every day.

Here is my ask & prayer. Both of you know where I came from, and I know both of you have done enough already, but I realize that I need you both to continue progressing. If I slip and mess up and show signs of the old me, please go easy on me!

Final Thoughts:

Females:

You are powerful; you can impact a man in a way that can lead to him changing the world. Once

God reveals to you your husband and possibly even shows you his potential, go easy on him. If God sent him, you will reap the reward if you faint not.

Males:

We have arrived, listen and get better every day. Continue to strive to be a kingdom man, continue to pray that the Lord takes away everything that is not of him, that he heals everything that has you broken; your victory is waiting on you, and you will reap if you faint not.

How Am I Better

I honestly didn't feel like I deserved to be healed after all I had done, but the LORD waited on me, and I am thankful for your grace God. I often find myself blissful thinking about how God could use someone like me to spread his word. To be an example of how he can completely change someone around. As I began to feel the pieces of me being put back together, I have a new peace. My strength is also renewed, my purpose is clearer, and my soul has been delivered.

I AM NO LONGER BROKEN BUT STRONG IN THE LORD!

As I walk in my new strength, I recognize the attacks of the enemy clearer. I don't easily fall victim to his tricks and persuasions like I did in my past because I am mentally stronger.

As I overcome the positions and the pains of being broken, I am encouraged, encouraged because I have a new type of power. A power that forces me to want to do more for the LORD because he has truly been amazing to me. That same power pushes me to want to help others overcome their brokenness, helping them understand that if he did it for me, he will and can do it for them too. When I thought I could not take anymore, you were always there. Your presence has allowed me to gain the patience and courage to endure. That has caused me to become physically stronger.

At my lowest position, I saw your face. Your love for me has changed the way I love others. It caused me to realize that pursuing after you first is the only answer. I am forever committed to seeking your face because I am now spiritually stronger.

NO ONE COMPARES TO YOU; YOU ARE SO AMAZING!

Final Thought:

What Will Your Legacy Be
(part 2)

What will your legacy be? When it's all said and done, and others are looking back at your memory, what will they see? Did you stay in your defeat and allow your brokenness to restrict you from finding and walking in your purpose? Did you find comfort in being the victim because the road to victory seemed too far away? Have those connected to you become better? Will you have accomplished your dreams while helping others fulfill theirs, or will you be considered a dream killer? What was most satisfying to you, only being filled or pouring into others and filling them as well? Will your immature decisions burden your family, or will you have things in order that will strengthen your legacy?

You get to control your legacy. No person, place, or thing has the ability to stop you but you. Do what is necessary for you to be no longer called or feel broken. No matter your past, don't give up on yourself. Pray and ask the LORD to make you complete and follow his direction.

Your peace and the ability to be mentally, physically, and most importantly, spiritually stronger will be the result of that prayer.

I BELIEVE IN YOU!

I pray that you have enjoyed reading Diary of a Broken Man.

Please scan the QR code below to connect on social media and retrieve my contact information.

I ask that you also use the code to leave your review of this book on Amazon.com.

I look forward to connecting with you

STAY CONNECTED

www.ingramcontent.com/pod-product-compliance
Lightning Source LLC
Chambersburg PA
CBHW072157160426
43197CB00012B/2421